Harcourt

MATH
Expressions
Common Core

Dr. Karen C. Fuson

GRADE

K

Volume 2

This material is based upon work supported by the
National Science Foundation
under Grant Numbers
ESI-9816320, REC-9806020, and RED-935373.

Any opinions, findings, and conclusions, or recommendations expressed in this material
are those of the author and do not necessarily reflect the views of the National Science Foundation.

VOLUME 2 CONTENTS

UNIT 4 Partners, Problem Drawings, and Tens

* This lesson consists only of activities from the Teacher Edition.

VOLUME 2 CONTENTS *(continued)*

© Houghton Mifflin Harcourt Publishing Company

* This lesson consists only of activities from the Teacher Edition.

UNIT 5 Consolidation of Concepts

VOLUME 2 CONTENTS *(continued)*

* This lesson consists only of activities from the Teacher Edition.

4-1 Class Activity

Name

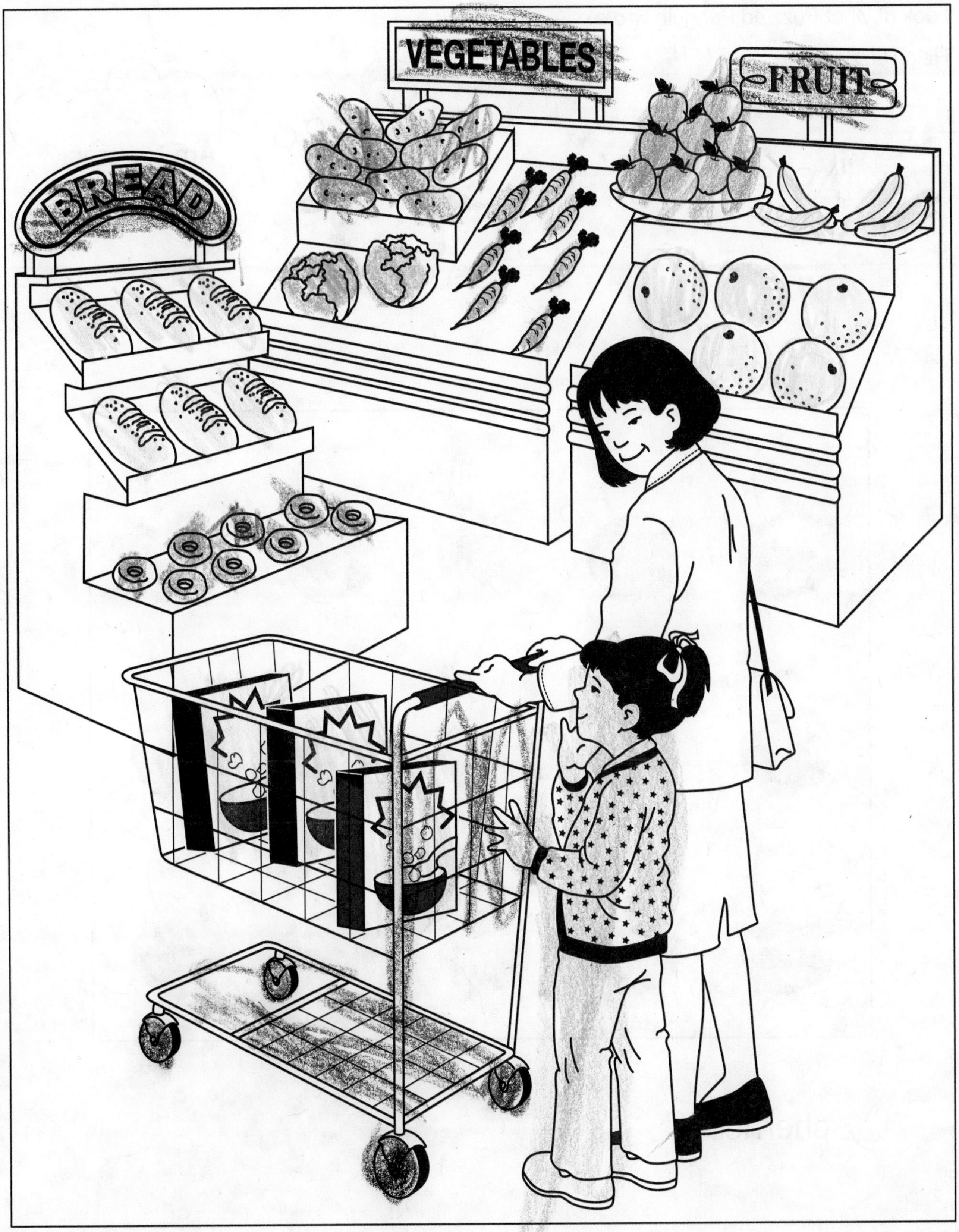

Name _____

Look at what Puzzled Penguin wrote.

Help Puzzled Penguin.

1̸4 cherries

Am I correct?

1̸5 cherries

Numbers 1–10 and Math Stories: Grocery Store Scenario

Cut on the dashed lines.

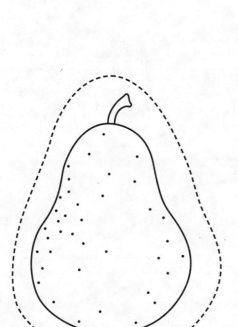

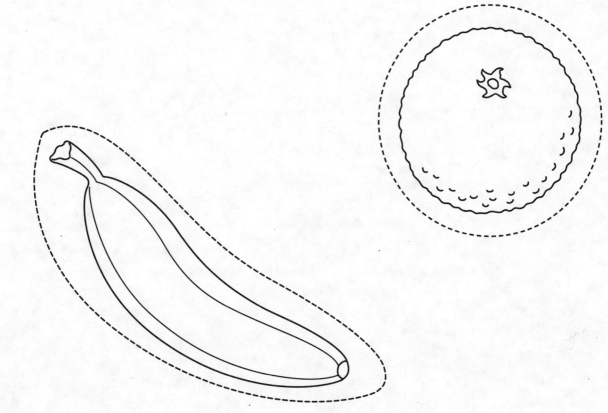

Fruit

Cut on the dashed lines.

Vegetables **155**

Vegetables

VOCABULARY
partners

1. Draw a line to show the **partners**. Then write the partners.

$$10 = \boxed{1} + \boxed{9}$$

$$10 = \boxed{2} + \boxed{8}$$

$$10 = \boxed{3} + \boxed{7}$$

$$10 = \boxed{4} + \boxed{6}$$

$$10 = \boxed{5} + \boxed{5}$$

$$10 = \boxed{6} + \boxed{4}$$

$$10 = \boxed{7} + \boxed{3}$$

$$10 = \boxed{8} + \boxed{2}$$

$$10 = \boxed{9} + \boxed{1}$$

Name _____

2. Show and write the partners. Begin with 9 + 1.

$10 = \boxed{9} + \boxed{1}$

$10 = \boxed{8} + \boxed{2}$

$10 = \boxed{7} + \boxed{3}$

$10 = \boxed{6} + \boxed{4}$

$10 = \boxed{5} + \boxed{5}$

$10 = \boxed{4} + \boxed{6}$

$10 = \boxed{3} + \boxed{7}$

$10 = \boxed{2} + \boxed{8}$

$10 = \boxed{1} + \boxed{9}$

Find Partners of 10

Name _____

Set A

11 = 10 + 1	12 = 10 + 2	13 = 10 + 3	14 = 10 + 4	15 = 10 + 5
16 = 10 + 6	17 = 10 + 7	18 = 10 + 8	19 = 10 + 9	20 = 10 + 10

Set B

10 + 1 = 11	10 + 2 = 12	10 + 3 = 13	10 + 4 = 14	10 + 5 = 15
10 + 6 = 16	10 + 7 = 17	10 + 8 = 18	10 + 9 = 19	10 + 10 = 20

Teen Equation Cards

1. Show the partners with fingers. Then write the total.

$10 + 1 = \boxed{11}$ $10 + 6 = \boxed{16}$

$10 + 2 = \boxed{12}$ $10 + 7 = \boxed{17}$

$10 + 3 = \boxed{13}$ $10 + 8 = \boxed{18}$

$10 + 4 = \boxed{14}$ $10 + 9 = \boxed{19}$

$10 + 5 = \boxed{15}$

2. Write the numbers 1–20.

1	2	3	4	5	6	7	8	9	10
11	12	13	14	15	16	17	18	19	20

3. Draw a picture to show 10 ones and 2 ones.

© Houghton Mifflin Harcourt Publishing Company

PATH to
FLUENCY

4. Subtract the numbers. Use your fingers or draw.

3 – 2 = 1   5 – 5 = 0   2 – 2 = 0

4 – 1 = 3   4 – 3 = 1   3 – 1 = 2

3 – 3 = 0   5 – 2 = 3   4 – 3 = 1

5 – 0 = 5   4 – 2 = 2   3 – 0 = 3

2 – 1 = 1   5 – 4 = 1   5 – 3 = 2

5. Choose an equation. Draw a picture to show the subtraction. Write the equation.

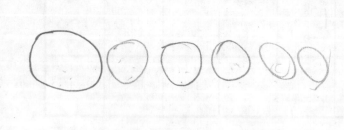

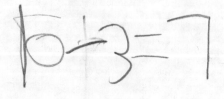

10 – 3 = 7

Teen Numbers and Equations

Family Letter

Dear Family:

Throughout the year, your child will be learning how to "break apart" numbers. For example, 6 equals 5 and 1, 4 and 2, and 3 and 3. We call two numbers that add up to a number the *partners* of the number.

To strengthen your child's understanding of these concepts, you can play *The Unknown Partner Game* with him or her. The game is played as follows:

Put out 5 objects such as buttons or crackers. Count them together. Have your child cover his or her eyes while you take a partner away. Ask your child to tell you the missing amount. Now it is your turn to close your eyes!

You can play this game again and again, starting with a different total each time. Start with 5 first (because it is easiest), and then move on to 6, 7, 8, 9, and 10.

Thank you!

Sincerely,
Your child's teacher

COMMON CORE

Unit 4 includes the Common Core Standards for Mathematical Content for Counting and Cardinality K.CC.1, K.CC.3, K.CC.4a, K.CC.4b, K.CC.4c, K.CC.5, K.CC.6, K.CC.7; Operations and Algebraic Thinking K.OA.1, K.OA.2, K.OA.3, K.OA.4, K.OA.5; Number and Operations in Base Ten K.NBT.1; Measurement and Data K.MD.3; Geometry K.G.1, K.G.2, K.G.5, K.G.6 and all Mathematical Practices.

Estimada familia:

Durante todo el año su niño aprenderá a "separar" números. Por ejemplo, 6 es igual a 5 más 1, 4 más 2, y 3 más 3. A dos números que sumados dan como resultado otro número los llamamos *partes* del número.

Puede jugar al juego de las partes desconocidas con su niño para reforzar estas ideas. Se juega de esta manera:

Coloque en algún lugar 5 objetos, como botones o galletas. Cuéntenlos juntos. Pida a su niño que se tape los ojos mientras Ud. quita una parte. Pida a su niño que diga la cantidad que falta. ¡Ahora es su turno de cerrar los ojos!

Jueguen varias veces, siempre empezando con un total diferente. Empiecen con 5 (por ser el más fácil) y sigan con 6, 7, 8, 9 y 10.

¡Gracias!

Atentamente,
El maestro de su niño

COMMON CORE La Unidad 4 incluye los Common Core Standards for Mathematical Content for Counting and Cardinality K.CC.1, K.CC.3, K.CC.4a, K.CC.4b, K.CC.4c, K.CC.5, K.CC.6, K.CC.7; Operations and Algebraic Thinking K.OA.1, K.OA.2, K.OA.3, K.OA.4, K.OA.5; Number and Operations in Base Ten K.NBT.1; Measurement and Data K.MD.3; Geometry K.G.1, K.G.2, K.G.5, K.G.6 and all Mathematical Practices.

Practice with Teen Numbers and Partners

Name _____

Draw lines to match. Circle the **extras**.

Write the numbers and compare them.

Write G for **Greater** and L for **Less**.

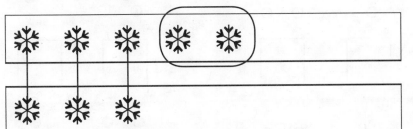 5   G

3   L

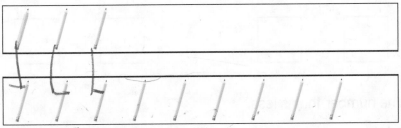 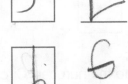
3   L

6   6

4   6

2   L

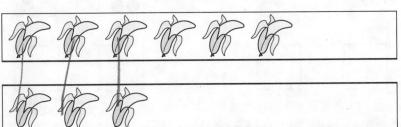 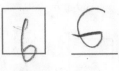
6   6

3   L

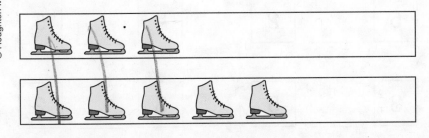 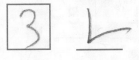
3   L

5   6

VOCABULARY
greater than
less than

Count and write the number. Circle the number that is greater.

(**3**) **2**

☐ ☐   ☐ ☐

☐ ☐   ☐ ☐

Count and write the number. Circle the number that is less.

☐ ☐   ☐ ☐

☐ ☐   ☐ ☐

Compare the numbers. Write G for **Greater than** or L for **Less than**.

| 2 | L | 3 | | 5 | ___ | 2 | | 4 | ___ | 5 |

| 4 | ___ | 1 | | 3 | ___ | 5 | | 3 | ___ | 2 |

Count, Match, and Compare

Draw a line to show two **partners**. Write the partners.

10 = ☐ + ☐   10 = ☐ + ☐

10 = ☐ + ☐   10 = ☐ + ☐

10 = ☐ + ☐   10 = ☐ + ☐

10 = ☐ + ☐   10 = ☐ + ☐

10 = ☐ + ☐

Name _____

Draw Tiny Tumblers on the Math Mountains.

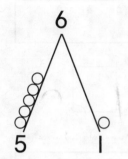
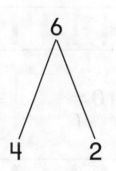
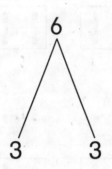
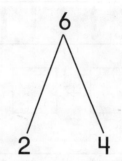
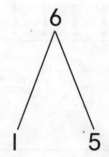

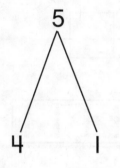
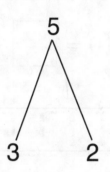
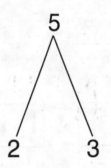
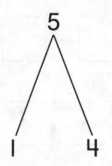
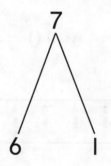

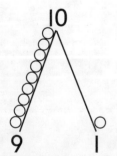
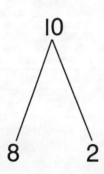
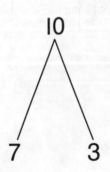

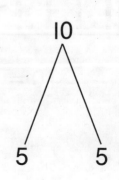

Break-Apart Numbers for 10

Name _____

Write the numbers 1–20.

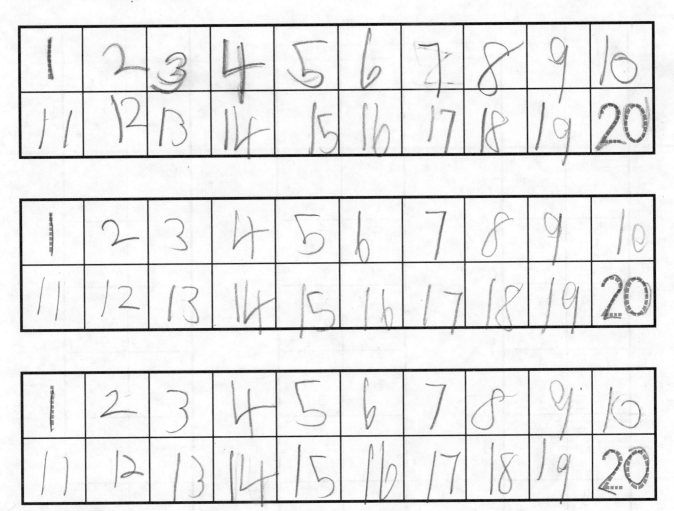

1	2	3	4	5	6	7	8	9	10
11	12	13	14	15	16	17	18	19	20

1	2	3	4	5	6	7	8	9	10
11	12	13	14	15	16	17	18	19	20

1	2	3	4	5	6	7	8	9	10
11	12	13	14	15	16	17	18	19	20

Count how many.

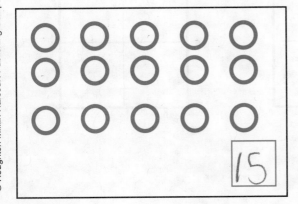

15

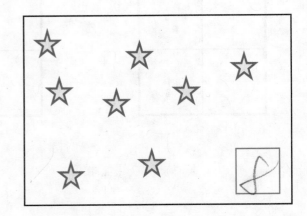

Write the numbers 1–20.

1	11
2	12
3	13
4	14
5	15
6	16
7	17
8	18
9	19
10	20

1	11
2	12
3	13
4	14
5	15
6	16
7	17
8	18
9	19
10	20

1	11
2	12
3	13
4	14
5	15
6	16
7	17
8	18
9	19
10	20

Break-Apart Numbers for 10

Name

1. Count and write the number. Circle the number that is **greater**.

(4) 2   3 (5)   (5) 3

2 (5)   2 (3)   (5) 4

2. Count and write the number. Circle the number that is **less**.

5 (4)   4 (3)   5 (3)

(2) 3   4 (3)   (4) 5

3. Write the numbers 1 through 20 in order.

1	2	3	4	5	6	7	8	9	10
11	12	13	14	15	16	17	18	19	20

Addition and Subtraction Drawings: Grocery Store Scenario **171**

Name _____

4. Draw lines to match. Circle the **extras**.

Write the numbers and compare them.

Write G for **Greater than** and L for **Less than**.

   6 G

 4 L

   3 L

 5 G

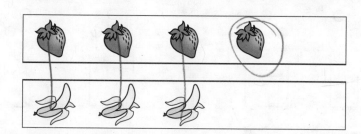   4 G

 3 L

   2 L

 5 G

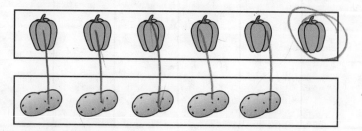   6 G

 5 L

Addition and Subtraction Drawings: Grocery Store Scenario

Name _____

I. Draw a line to show the **partners**. Write the partners.

10 = ⬚1⬚ + ⬚9⬚   10 = ⬚2⬚ + ⬚8⬚

10 = ⬚3⬚ + ⬚7⬚   10 = ⬚4⬚ + ⬚6⬚

10 = ⬚5⬚ + ⬚5⬚   10 = ⬚6⬚ + ⬚4⬚

10 = ⬚7⬚ + ⬚3⬚   10 = ⬚8⬚ + ⬚2⬚

10 = ⬚9⬚ + ⬚1⬚

2. Draw Tiny Tumblers on the Math Mountains.

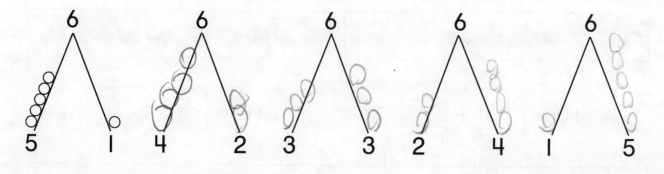

6 · 5 · 1
6 · 4 · 2
6 · 3 · 3
6 · 2 · 4
6 · 1 · 5

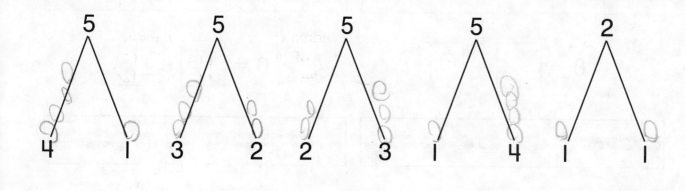

5 · 4 · 1
5 · 3 · 2
5 · 2 · 3
5 · 1 · 4
2 · 1 · 1

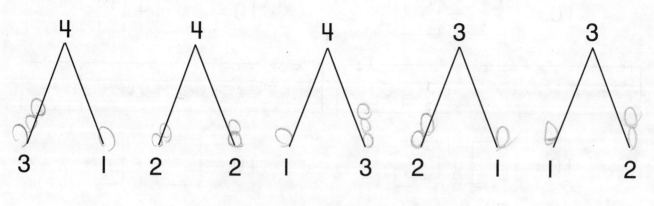

4 · 3 · 1
4 · 2 · 2
4 · 1 · 3
3 · 2 · 1
3 · 1 · 2

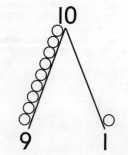
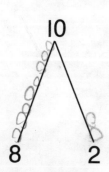
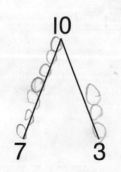
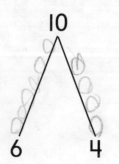
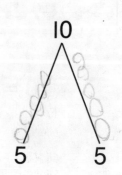

10 · 9 · 1
10 · 8 · 2
10 · 7 · 3
10 · 6 · 4
10 · 5 · 5

Partners of 10 with 5-Groups

VOCABULARY
add

1. **Add** the numbers.

$5 + 1 =$ 6 $4 + 2 =$ 6 $3 + 3 =$ 6

$6 + 1 =$ 7 $5 + 2 =$ 7 $4 + 3 =$ 7

$7 + 1 =$ 8 $6 + 2 =$ 8 $5 + 3 =$ 8

$8 + 1 =$ 9 $7 + 2 =$ 9 $6 + 3 =$ 9

$9 + 1 =$ 10 $8 + 2 =$ 10 $7 + 3 =$ 10

2. Connect the dots in order.

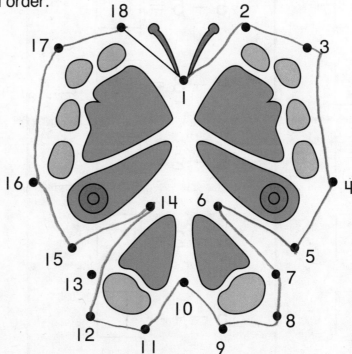

3. Add the numbers.

$2 + 3 =$ 5 $0 + 2 =$ 2 $3 + 1 =$ 4

$4 + 0 =$ 5 $2 + 1 =$ 3 $1 + 1 =$ 2

$5 + 0 =$ 6 $1 + 2 =$ 3 $0 + 3 =$ 3

$3 + 1 =$ 4 $1 + 4 =$ 5 $1 + 3 =$ 4

$3 + 2 =$ 5 $2 + 2 =$ 4 $4 + 1 =$ 5

4. Subtract the numbers.

$3 - 2 =$ 1 $5 - 5 =$ 0 $2 - 2 =$ 0

$4 - 1 =$ 3 $4 - 3 =$ 1 $3 - 1 =$ 2

$3 - 3 =$ 0 $5 - 2 =$ 3 $5 - 1 =$ 4

$5 - 0 =$ 5 $4 - 2 =$ 2 $3 - 0 =$ 3

$2 - 1 =$ 1 $5 - 4 =$ 1 $5 - 3 =$ 2

Addition Equations

Name

VOCABULARY
Tiny Tumblers
Math Mountains

1. Draw **Tiny Tumblers** ... the **Math Mountains**.

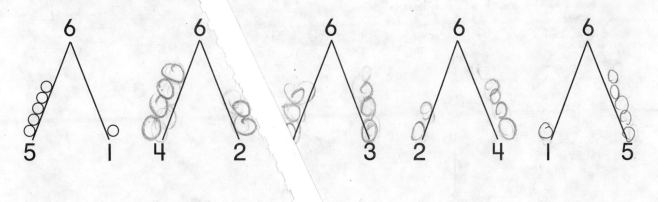

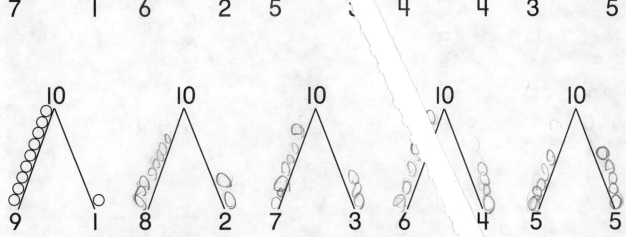

2. Write the numbers 1 through 20.

1	2	3	4	5	6	7	8		10
11	12	13	14	15	16	17	18		20

Name

Help Kate find the gate.

3. She needs to find the partners of 8.

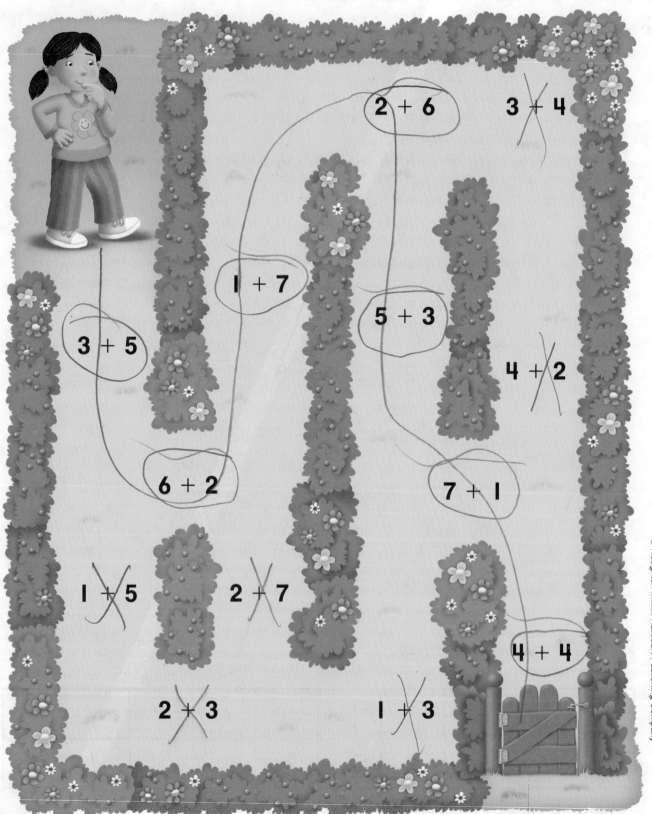

More Partners of 10 with 5-Groups

VOCABULARY
add

I. **Add** the numbers.

5 + 5 = ☐ 10

6 + 2 = ☐ 8

2 + 7 = ☐ 9

3 + 4 = ☐ 7

4 + 2 = ☐ 6

7 + 3 = ☐ 10

5 + 1 = ☐ 6

4 + 4 = ☐ 8

5 + 4 = ☐ 9

3 + 6 = ☐ 9

5 + 2 = ☐ 7

5 + 3 = ☐ 8

4 + 6 = ☐ 10

3 + 3 = ☐ 6

2 + 5 = ☐ 7

2. Connect the dots in order.

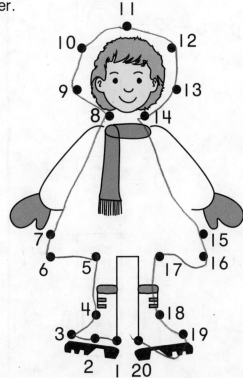

3. Add the numbers.

4 + 1 = 5

3 + 2 = 5

5 + 0 = 5

2 + 2 = 4

2 + 1 = 3

0 + 3 = 3

1 + 4 = 5

3 + 1 = 4

1 + 2 = 3

3 + 0 = 3

4 + 0 = 4

1 + 1 = 2

1 + 3 = 4

0 + 5 = 5

2 + 3 = 5

4. Subtract the numbers.

5 − 4 = 1

4 − 4 = 0

3 − 1 = 2

2 − 1 = 1

1 − 0 = 0

5 − 2 = 3

4 − 2 = 2

3 − 0 = 3

2 − 2 = 0

1 − 1 = 0

5 − 1 = 4

4 − 3 = 1

3 − 3 = 0

2 − 0 = 2

5 − 3 = 2

Addition and Subtraction Equations

11

11

10 + 1 = 11

12

12

10 + 2 = 12

13

13

10 + 3 = 13

14

14

10 + __ = __

Name _____

1. Draw lines to match.

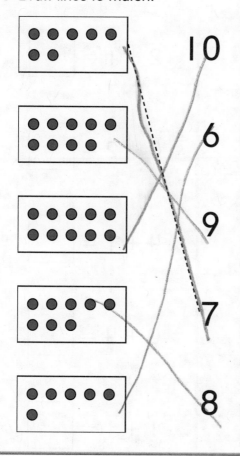

	10
	6
	9
	7
	8

2. Make two matches.

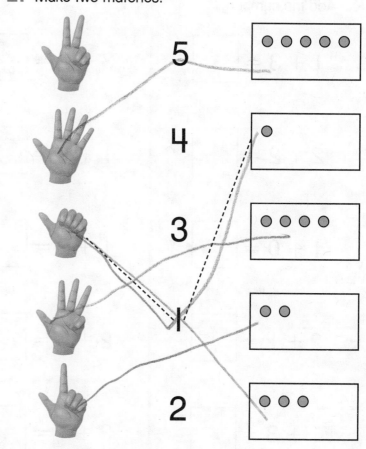

5	
4	
3	
1	
2	

3. Connect the dots in order.

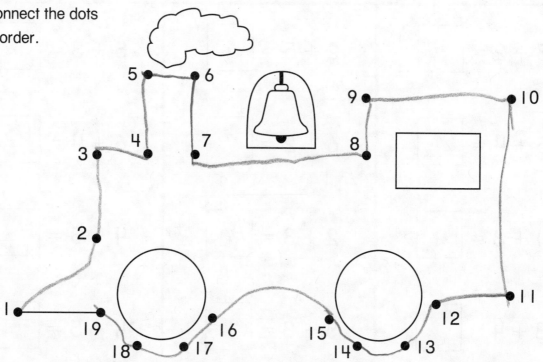

4. Add the numbers.

1 + 3 = 4   3 + 2 = 5   2 + 1 = 3

2 + 2 = 4   1 + 4 = 5   0 + 2 = 2

1 + 0 = 1   1 + 2 = 3   4 + 1 = 5

2 + 1 = 3   2 + 0 = 2   0 + 4 = 4

1 + 3 = 4   3 + 1 = 4   1 + 1 = 2

8 + 2 = 10   2 + 5 = 7   5 + 3 = 8

5 + 4 = 9   6 + 2 = 8   6 + 4 = 10

4 + 3 = 7   2 + 8 = 10   4 + 3 = 7

3 + 4 = 7   5 + 3 = 8   4 + 5 = 9

Teen Number Book

Name _____

VOCABULARY
add

PATH to
FLUENCY

1. **Add** the numbers.

3 + 1 = ☐

2 + 2 = ☐

0 + 4 = ☐

3 + 2 = ☐

5 + 0 = ☐

4 + 1 = ☐

2 + 0 = ☐

2 + 3 = ☐

0 + 1 = ☐

2 + 1 = ☐

3 + 0 = ☐

1 + 2 = ☐

0 + 5 = ☐

1 + 4 = ☐

1 + 3 = ☐

2. Connect the dots in order.

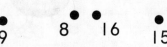

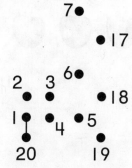

3. Subtract the numbers.

3 − 2 = ☐

5 − 5 = ☐

2 − 2 = ☐

4 − 1 = ☐

4 − 3 = ☐

3 − 1 = ☐

3 − 3 = ☐

5 − 2 = ☐

4 − 3 = ☐

5 − 0 = ☐

4 − 2 = ☐

3 − 0 = ☐

2 − 1 = ☐

5 − 4 = ☐

5 − 3 = ☐

4. Look at what Puzzled Penguin wrote.

Help Puzzled Penguin.

4 + 1 = 3

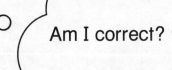
Am I correct?

4   +   1

4 + 1 = ____

VOCABULARY
partner equation

1. Write the **partner equation.**

$3 = 2 + 1$

$3 = 2 + 1$

$4 = 3 + 1$

$4 = 2 + 2$

$4 = 1 + 3$

$5 = 4 + 1$

$5 = 3 + 2$

$5 = 2 + 3$

$5 = 1 + 4$

$6 = 5 + 1$

$6 = 4 + 2$

$6 = 3 + 3$

$6 = 2 + 4$

$6 = 1 + 5$

$10 = 9 + 1$

$10 = 8 + 2$

$10 = 7 + 3$

$10 = 6 + 4$

$10 = 5 + 5$

$10 = 4 + 6$

$10 = 3 + 7$

$10 = 2 + 8$

$10 = 1 + 9$

Name _____

PATH to
FLUENCY

2. Add the numbers.

2 + 2 = ☐   3 + 0 = ☐   2 + 3 = ☐

3 + 1 = ☐   2 + 1 = ☐   1 + 0 = ☐

1 + 2 = ☐   0 + 4 = ☐   3 + 2 = ☐

4 + 1 = ☐   1 + 1 = ☐   0 + 2 = ☐

1 + 3 = ☐   2 + 1 = ☐   5 + 0 = ☐

3 + 4 = ☐   3 + 3 = ☐   5 + 3 = ☐

2 + 4 = ☐   3 + 5 = ☐   6 + 2 = ☐

1 + 5 = ☐   3 + 6 = ☐   8 + 2 = ☐

5 + 2 = ☐   1 + 9 = ☐   5 + 4 = ☐

Partners and Equations

4-18

Class Activity

Name ____________________

1 5

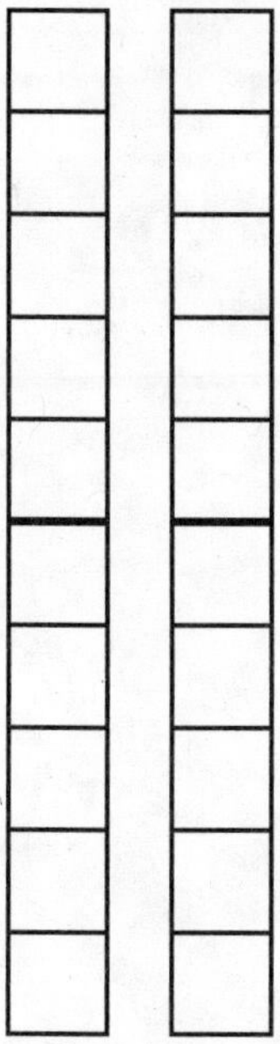

15

___

___

___

___

___

10 + __ = __

1 6

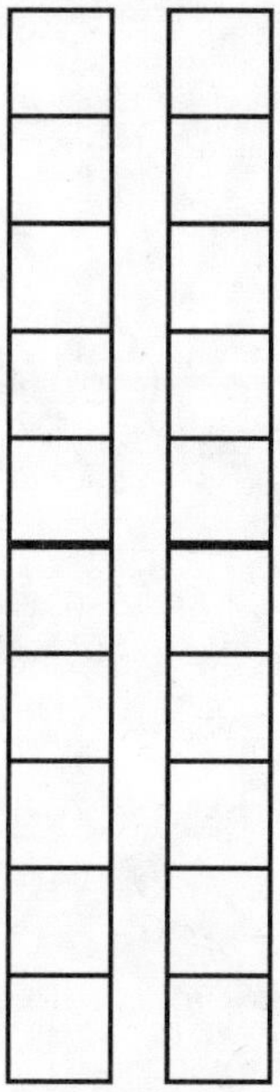

16

___

___

___

___

___

10 + __ = __

1 7

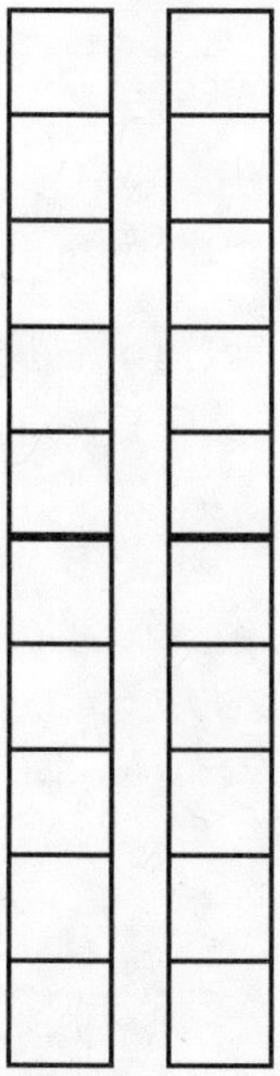

17

___

___

___

___

___

10 + __ = __

1 8

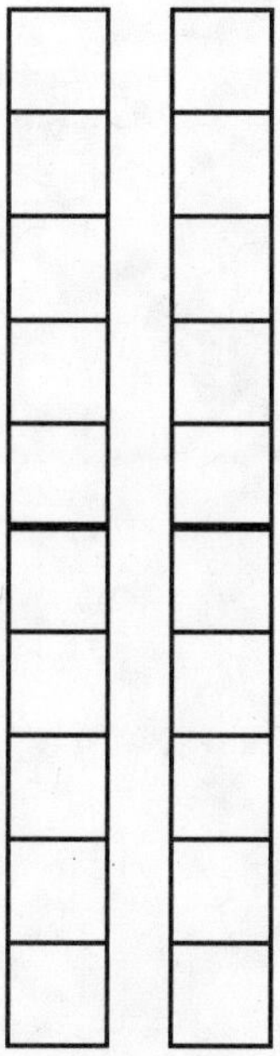

18

___

___

___

___

___

10 + __ = __

1. Write the partner equation.

| | 3 = 1 + 2 |
| | 4 = 1 + 3 |

| | _____ |
| | _____ |

	5 = 1 + 4
	_____
	_____
	_____

	10 = 1 + 9
	_____
	_____

	6 = 1 + 5
	_____
	_____
	_____
	_____
	_____

2. Subtract the numbers.

9 − 1 = ☐   8 − 1 = ☐   9 − 5 = ☐

10 − 4 = ☐   9 − 2 = ☐   7 − 2 = ☐

10 − 3 = ☐   8 − 4 = ☐   6 − 1 = ☐

7 − 4 = ☐   6 − 5 = ☐   10 − 2 = ☐

6 − 3 = ☐   6 − 4 = ☐   8 − 2 = ☐

3. Look at what Puzzled Penguin wrote.

Help Puzzled Penguin.

6 = 4 − 2

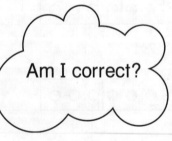

Am I correct?

Write Addition Equations

19

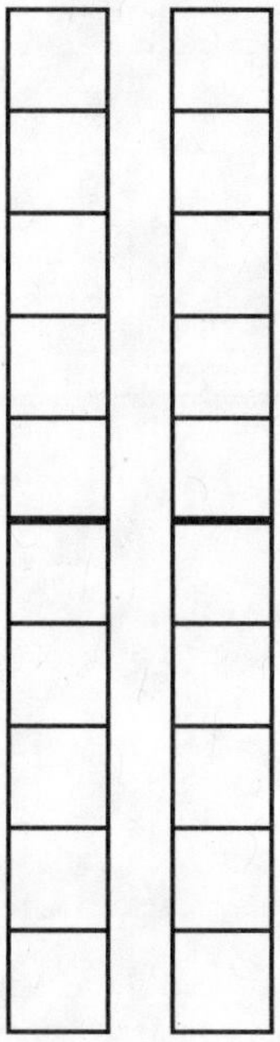

_19_
___
___
___
___
___
___
___

10 + ___ = ___

2 0

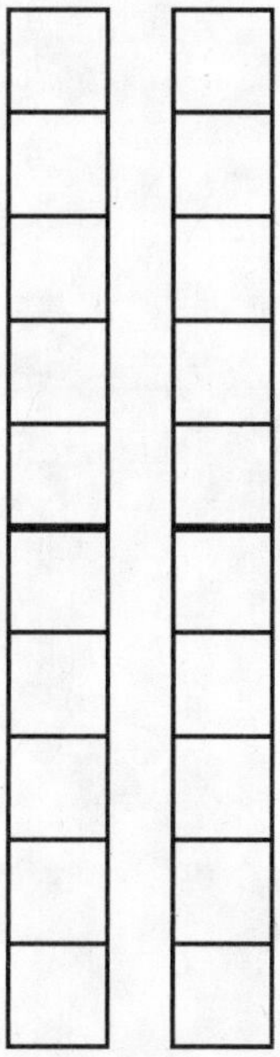

_20_
___
___
___
___
___
___
___

10 + ___ = ___

My

Unit 4

Teen Number

Book

By _____

↖ Fold here.

Name _____

1. Draw lines to match.

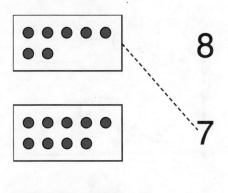

8

7

9

6

10

2. Make two matches.

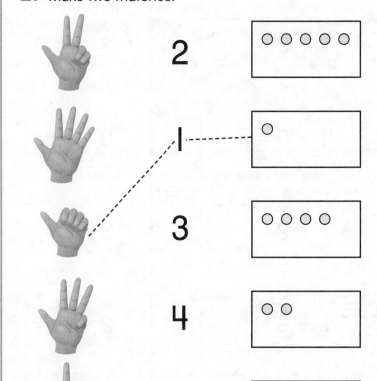

2

1

3

4

5

3. Count and write the number. Circle the number that is less.

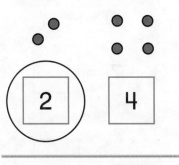

(2)   4

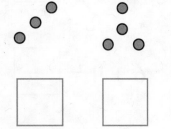

☐   ☐

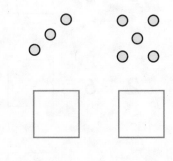

☐   ☐

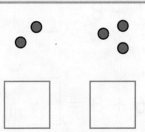

☐   ☐

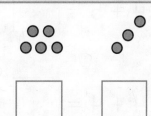

☐   ☐

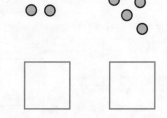

☐   ☐

4. Add the numbers.

1 + 3 = ☐   3 + 1 = ☐   5 + 0 = ☐

4 + 0 = ☐   0 + 2 = ☐   2 + 1 = ☐

1 + 2 = ☐   3 + 2 = ☐   2 + 3 = ☐

1 + 4 = ☐   2 + 2 = ☐   1 + 1 = ☐

2 + 1 = ☐   1 + 2 = ☐   4 + 1 = ☐

5 + 3 = ☐   5 + 1 = ☐   8 + 2 = ☐

2 + 6 = ☐   6 + 4 = ☐   3 + 7 = ☐

6 + 1 = ☐   4 + 5 = ☐   1 + 8 = ☐

3 + 7 = ☐   4 + 4 = ☐   6 + 3 = ☐

Teen Number Book

1. Circle the objects shaped like cubes on the top shelf. Circle the objects shaped like cylinders on the middle shelf. Circle the objects shaped like spheres on the bottom shelf.

2. Color each kind of shape.

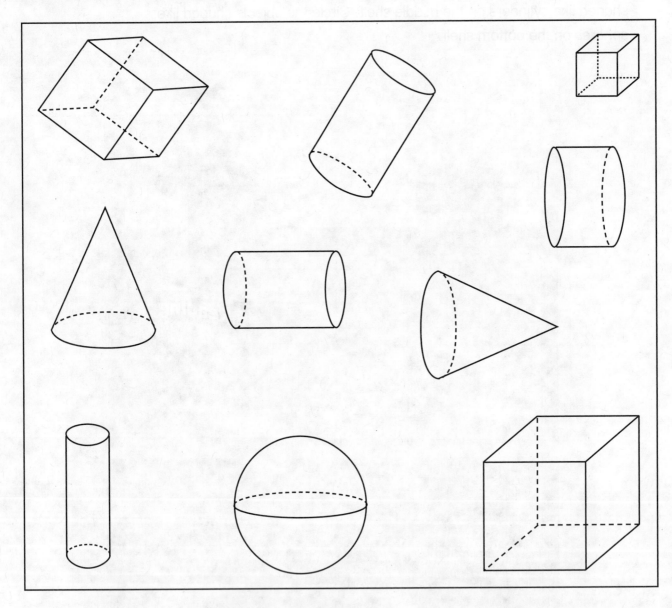

green

red

yellow

blue

Name _____

Exercises 1–2. Write the partners.

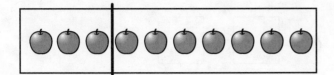 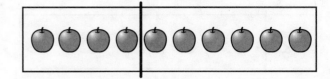

10 = ☐ + ☐   10 = ☐ + ☐

Exercise 3. Draw.

The store has 9 apples. Dad buys 3 apples. Draw the apples the store has now.

Exercises 4–6. Add the numbers.

3 + 2 = ☐   1 + 3 = ☐   2 + 1 = ☐

Exercises 7–9. Subtract the numbers.

4 − 3 = ☐   5 − 0 = ☐   3 − 1 = ☐

Exercises 10–11. Write the partners.

6 = ☐ + ☐

7 = ☐ + ☐

Exercises 12–13. Count and write the number. Circle the number that is less.

☐   ☐   ☐   ☐

Exercises 14–15. Complete the equation.

10 + 1 = ☐

10 + 6 = ☐

Exercises 16–17. Draw a line under the sphere. Circle the cone.

Exercise 18. Circle the cylinder that is next to the cube.

Exercise 19. Draw to show 15 as 10 ones and extra ones.

Name _____

Exercises 20–21. Add the numbers.

$8 + 2 =$ ⬜ $3 + 6 =$ ⬜

Exercises 22–23. Subtract the numbers.

$9 - 1 =$ ⬜ $7 - 4 =$ ⬜

Exercise 24. Write the partner equation.

| ● ● ● | ○ ○ | _____

Exercise 25. Extended Response Draw a picture that shows partners for 7.

Write the partner equation.

_____

Family Letter

Dear Family:

We are starting a new unit in math: Consolidation of Concepts. This unit builds on the concepts that were introduced in previous units. For example, children will be creating and solving simple story problems, and making shape pictures. Math projects will include making Teen Number Books and a Night Sky display with stars in groups of ten.

Special emphasis will be on the teen numbers. Here are some ways you can help your child understand teen numbers:

- Make a game of finding teen numbers on signs and in printed materials.
- Encourage your child to count everyday objects (groups of 11–19 items). Ask your child to regroup the objects to show ten ones and extra ones.
- Continue to assist your child with math homework pages.

Thank you!

Sincerely,
Your child's teacher

Unit 5 includes the Common Core Standards for Mathematical Content for Counting and Cardinality K.CC.1, K.CC.2, K.CC.3, K.CC.4, K.CC.4a, K.CC.4c, K.CC.5, K.CC.6, K.CC.7; Operations and Algebraic Thinking K.OA.1, K.OA.2, K.OA.3, K.OA.4, K.OA.5; Numbers and Operations in Base Ten K.NBT.1; Measurement and Data K.MD.1, K.MD.2

Estimada familia:

Vamos a empezar una nueva unidad de matemáticas: Reforzar conceptos. Esta unidad se basa en los conceptos que se han estudiado en las unidades anteriores. Por ejemplo, los niños formularán y resolverán problemas sencillos y harán dibujos de figuras. Los proyectos de matemáticas consistirán en hacer libros de los números de 11 a 19 y un cartel que muestra el cielo de noche con estrellas en grupos de diez.

Se pondrá especial énfasis en los números de 11 a 19. Aquí tiene algunas sugerencias para ayudar a su niño a entender estos números:

- Invente un juego para buscar números de 11 a 19 en letreros y en materiales impresos.
- Anime a su niño a contar objetos cotidianos (grupos de 11 a 19 objetos). Pídale que reagrupe los objetos para mostrar, en cada caso, un grupo de diez unidades y otro grupo con las unidades que sobren.
- Siga ayudando a su niño con la tarea de matemáticas.

¡Gracias!

Atentamente,
El maestro de su niño

COMMON CORE

La Unidad 5 incluye los Common Core Standards for Mathematical Content for Counting and Cardinality K.CC.2, K.CC.3, K.CC.4, K.CC.4a, K.CC.4c, K.CC.5, K.CC.6, K.CC.7; Operations and Algebraic Thinking K.OA.1, K.OA.2, K.OA.3, K.OA.4, K.OA.5; Numbers and Operations in Base Ten K.NBT.1; Measurement and Data K.MD.1, K.MD.2

Name _____

Count the stars. Write the number.

19 My Count	13 My Count	10 My Count
8 My Count	16 My Count	12 My Count

Help Puzzled Penguin.

Puzzled Penguin was asked to write three teen numbers.

Did Puzzled Penguin write the numbers correctly?

Did I make a mistake?

How can we help Puzzled Penguin write the correct numbers?

Write the correct numbers for Puzzled Penguin.

14   17   19

Partners of 10: Stars in the Night Sky

Dear Family:

It is important that your child learn to see the ten in teen numbers. Each teen number (11, 12, 13, 14, 15, 16, 17, 18, and 19) is made of ten ones and some "extra ones."

Please help your child at home with groups of 11–19 objects. Ask your child to show the group of ten ones, show the extra ones, and then write the number. Below are two ways to display 17 pieces of cereal in a group of ten and extra ones, shown with a sample dialogue about the cereal.

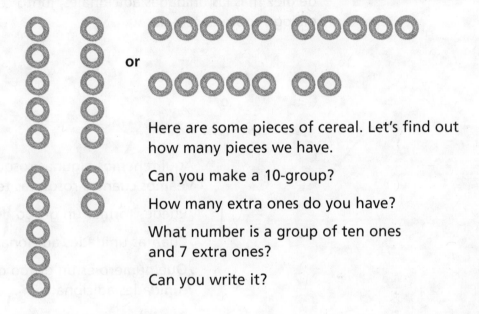

Here are some pieces of cereal. Let's find out how many pieces we have.

Can you make a 10-group?

How many extra ones do you have?

What number is a group of ten ones and 7 extra ones?

Can you write it?

If you have any questions or problems, please contact me. Thank you for your cooperation.

Sincerely,
Your child's teacher

© Houghton Mifflin Harcourt Publishing Company

COMMON CORE

Unit 5 includes the Common Core Standards for Mathematical Content for Counting and Cardinality K.CC.1, K.CC.2, K.CC.3, K.CC.4, K.CC.4a, K.CC.4c, K.CC.5, K.CC.6, K.CC.7; Operations and Algebraic Thinking K.OA.1, K.OA.2, K.OA.3, K.OA.4, K.OA.5; Numbers and Operations in Base Ten K.NBT.1; Measurement and Data K.MD.1, K.MD.2

Estimada familia:

Es importante que su niño aprenda a ver las decenas en los números de 11 a 19. Cada uno de estos números (11, 12, 13, 14, 15, 16, 17, 18 y 19) está formado por diez unidades más algunas "unidades adicionales".

Por favor, ayude a su niño en casa a formar grupos que tengan de 11 a 19 objetos. Pídale que muestre el grupo de diez unidades y las unidades adicionales, y que luego escriba el número. Abajo hay dos maneras de mostrar 17 rosquitas de cereal en un grupo de diez más las unidades adicionales, junto con un ejemplo de un diálogo sobre el cereal.

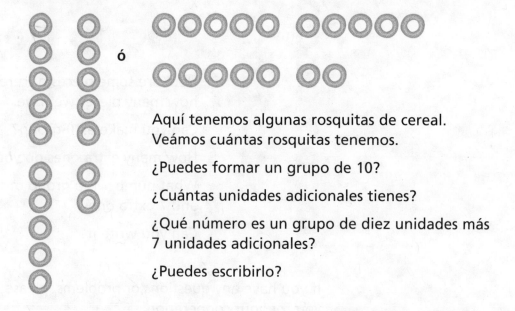

Aquí tenemos algunas rosquitas de cereal. Veámos cuántas rosquitas tenemos.

¿Puedes formar un grupo de 10?

¿Cuántas unidades adicionales tienes?

¿Qué número es un grupo de diez unidades más 7 unidades adicionales?

¿Puedes escribirlo?

Si tiene alguna duda o pregunta, por favor comuníquese conmigo. Gracias por su cooperación.

Atentamente,
El maestro de su niño

COMMON CORE

La Unidad 5 incluye los Common Core Standards for Mathematical Content for Counting and Cardinality K.CC.1, K.CC.2, K.CC.3, K.CC.4, K.CC.4a, K.CC.4c, K.CC.5, K.CC.6, K.CC.7; Operations and Algebraic Thinking K.OA.1, K.OA.2, K.OA.3, K.OA.4, K.OA.5; Numbers and Operations in Base Ten K.NBT.1; Measurement and Data K.MD.1, K.MD.2

More Partners of 10: Stars in the Night Sky

10 = 1 + 9

10 = 6 + 4

10 = 2 + 8

10 = 7 + 3

10 = 3 + 7

10 = 8 + 2

10 = 4 + 6

10 = 9 + 1

10 = 5 + 5

10 = 6 + 5

Name

Draw circles to show each number.
Write the ten and the ones under the circles.
Complete the equations on the bottom.

11	12	13	14	15	16	17	18	19	20
10 + 1	10 + 2	10 + 3	10 + 4	10 + 5	10 + 6	10 + 7	10 + 8	10 + 9	10 + 10

14 = 10 + 4

15 = 10 + 5

12 = 10 + 2

13 = 10 + 3

17 = 10 + 7

19 = 10 + 9

16 = 10 + 6

18 = 10 + 8

© Houghton Mifflin Harcourt Publishing Company

More Partners of 10: Stars in the Night Sky

Name _____

VOCABULARY
ten
one
equation

Circle the **ten** ones.

Write the ten ones and more **ones** in each **equation**.

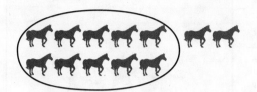

___10___ + ___2___ = ___12___

_____ + _____ = _____

_____ + _____ = _____

_____ + _____ = _____

_____ + _____ = _____

_____ + _____ = _____

_____ + _____ = _____

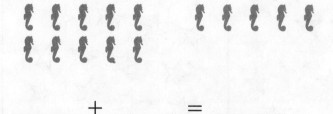

_____ + _____ = _____

_____ + _____ = _____

Solve and Retell Story Problems **215**

Count the stars. Write the number.

Solve and Retell Story Problems

Write the numbers 1–100 in vertical columns.

1	11	21							
2									
10									100

Write the numbers 1–100 in horizontal rows.

1	2								10
11									
21									
									100

Make Quantities 1–20

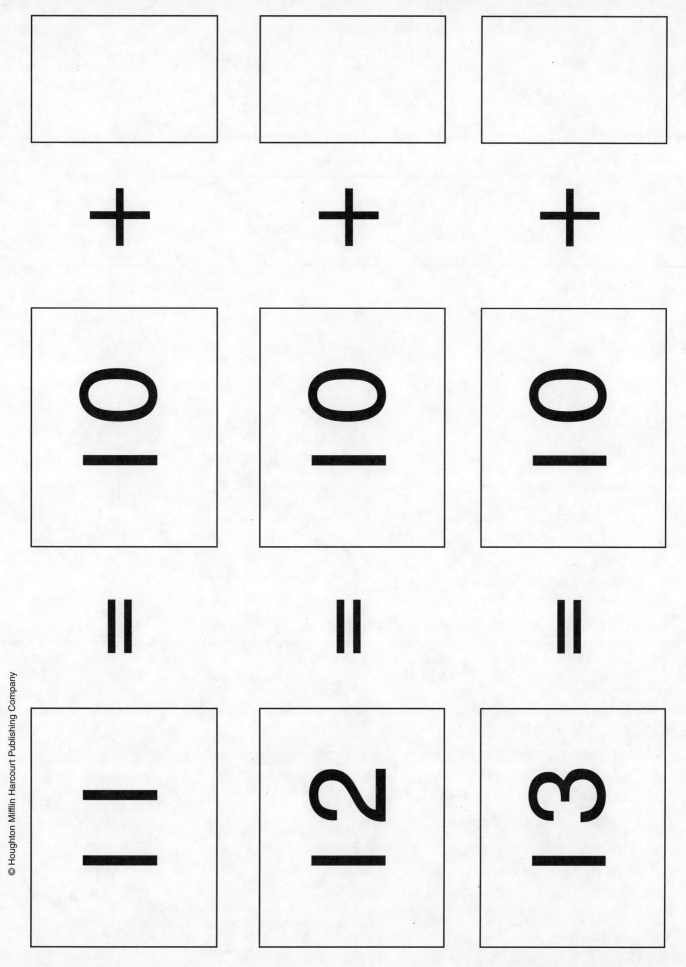

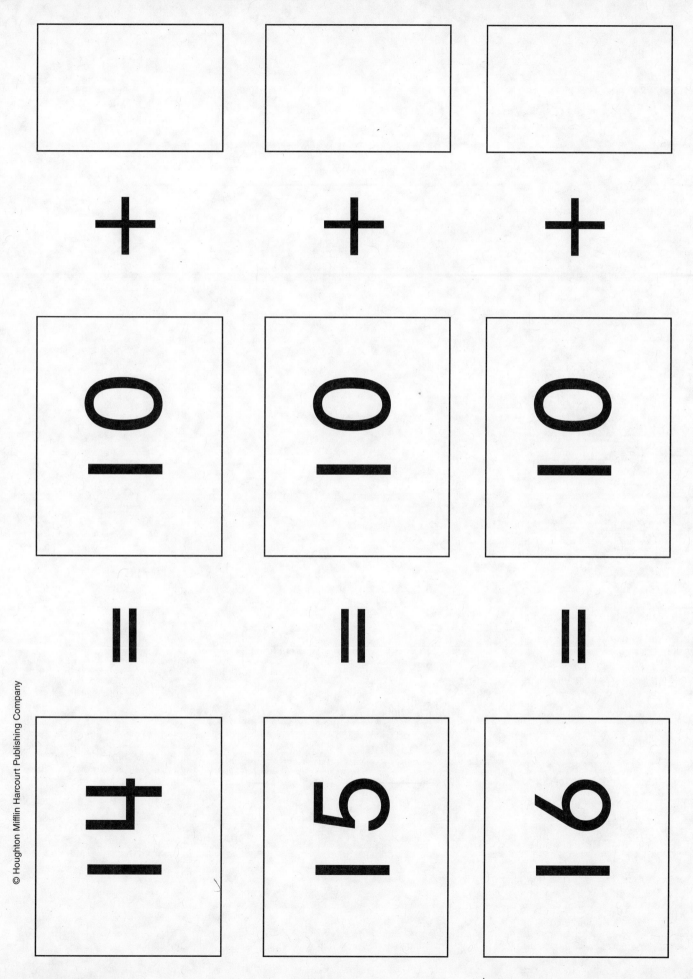

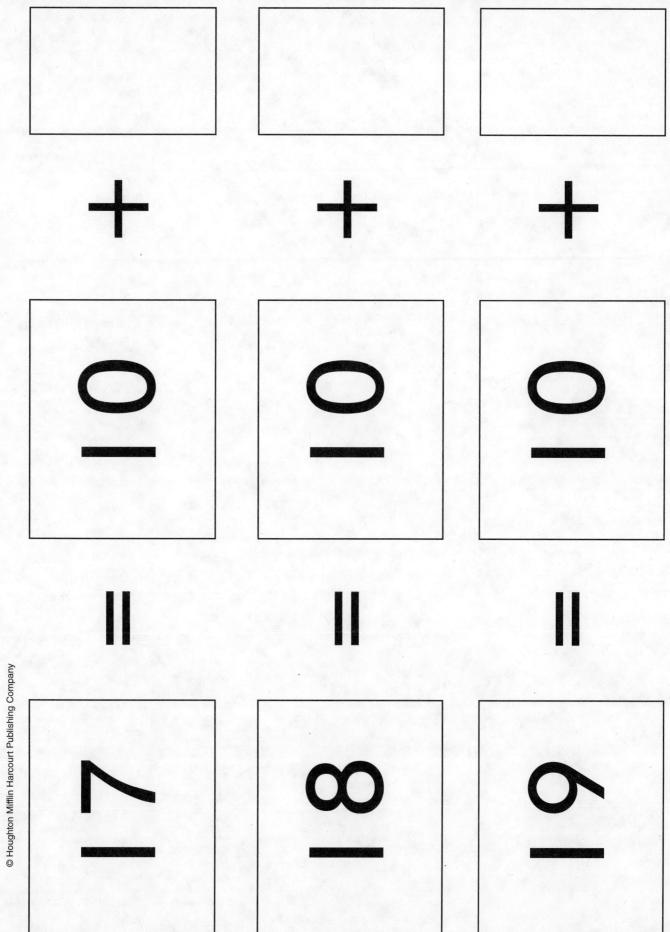

Name _____

5

VOCABULARY
partner

Write the 5- **partners**.

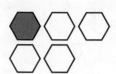

$1 + 4$

$2 + 3$

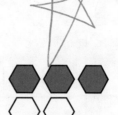

$3 + 2$

$4 + 1$

$1 + 4$

$2 + 3$

$3 + 2$

$4 + 1$

$1 + 4$

$2 + 3$

$3 + 2$

$4 + 1$

$1 + 4$

$2 + 3$

$3 + 2$

$4 + 1$

2 + 1 = ☐   3 + 1 = ☐   2 + 2 = ☐

2 + 3 = ☐   1 + 3 = ☐   3 + 2 = ☐

5 + 0 = ☐   4 + 1 = ☐   0 + 5 = ☐

3 + 1 = ☐   2 + 2 = ☐   1 + 4 = ☐

2 + 3 = ☐   1 + 1 = ☐   1 + 2 = ☐

5 − 1 = ☐   3 − 2 = ☐   4 − 4 = ☐

4 − 2 = ☐   5 − 3 = ☐   2 − 1 = ☐

2 − 2 = ☐   3 − 0 = ☐   5 − 4 = ☐

5 − 2 = ☐   4 − 3 = ☐   1 − 0 = ☐

4 − 1 = ☐   5 − 2 = ☐   3 − 1 = ☐

VOCABULARY
Tiny Tumbler
Math Mountain

Draw **Tiny Tumblers** on each **Math Mountain** and write the partner.

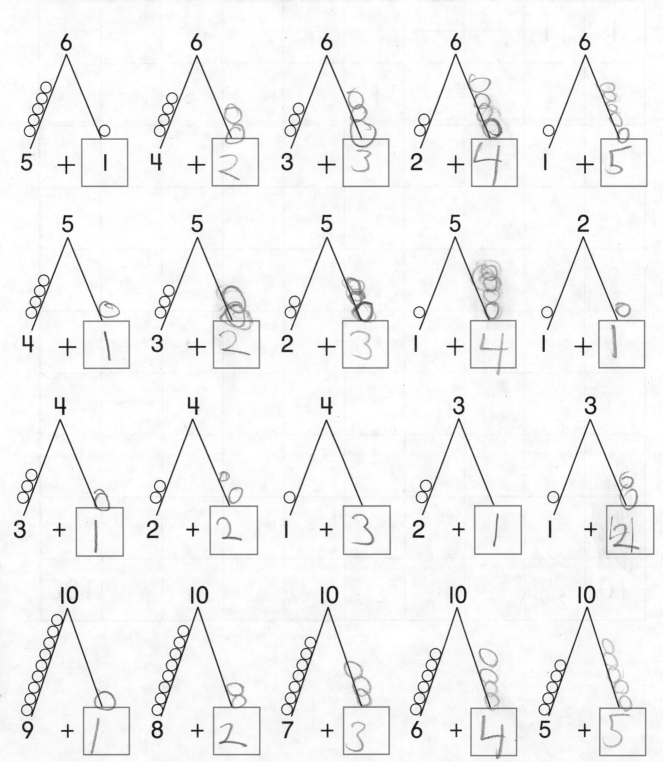

6
5 + 1

6
4 + 2

6
3 + 3

6
2 + 4

6
1 + 5

5
4 + 1

5
3 + 2

5
2 + 3

5
1 + 4

2
1 + 1

4
3 + 1

4
2 + 2

4
1 + 3

3
2 + 1

3
1 + 2

10
9 + 1

10
8 + 2

10
7 + 3

10
6 + 4

10
5 + 5

Name _____

Write the numbers 1–100.

1	11	21	31	41	51	61	71	81	91
2	12	22	32	42	52	62	72	82	92
3	13	73	33	43	53	63	73	83	93
4	14	24	34	44	54	64	74	84	94
5	15	25	35	45	55	65	75	85	95
6	16	26	36	46	56	66	76	86	96
7	17	27	37	47	57	67	77	87	97
8	18	28	38	48	58	68	78	88	98
9	19	29	39	49	59	69	79	89	99
10	20	30	40	50	60	70	80	90	100

Name _____

6

VOCABULARY
partner

Write the 6-**partners**.

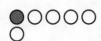

$1 + 5$ $2 + 4$ $3 + 3$ $4 + 2$ $5 + 1$

1+5   2+4   3+3   4+2   5+1

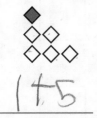      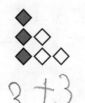   

1+5   2+4   3+3   4+2   5+1

1+5   2+4   3+3   4+2   5+1

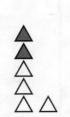   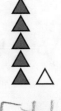

1+5   2+4   3+3   4+2   5+1

Name _____

Add the numbers.

1 + 1 = 2   1 + 4 = 5   2 + 1 = 3

1 + 0 = 1   3 + 2 = 5   4 + 1 = 5

2 + 2 = 4   2 + 1 = 3   3 + 0 = 3

2 + 3 = 5   1 + 2 = 3   3 + 1 = 4

1 + 1 = 2   2 + 2 = 4   1 + 3 = 4

1 + 8 = 9   3 + 3 = 6   7 + 3 = 10

6 + 2 = 8   4 + 3 = 7   4 + 6 = 10

6 + 4 = 10   4 + 4 = 8   5 + 1 = 6

5 + 5 = 10   4 + 5 = 9   6 + 2 = 8

Partners of 6, 7, 8, and 9

VOCABULARY
equal
unequal

PATH to
FLUENCY

Subtract the numbers. Use your fingers or draw.

$3 - 2 = \boxed{1}$ $5 - 5 = \boxed{0}$ $2 - 2 = \boxed{0}$

$4 - 1 = \boxed{3}$ $4 - 3 = \boxed{1}$ $3 - 1 = \boxed{2}$

$3 - 3 = \boxed{0}$ $5 - 2 = \boxed{3}$ $4 - 3 = \boxed{1}$

$5 - 0 = \boxed{5}$ $4 - 2 = \boxed{2}$ $3 - 0 = \boxed{3}$

$2 - 1 = \boxed{1}$ $5 - 4 = \boxed{1}$ $5 - 3 = \boxed{2}$

Write the symbol to show **equal** or **unequal**.

   $=$ or $\neq$

2 $\neq$ ●●	●● $=$ ✋(3)	10 $=$ 2 + 8
5 $=$ ●●●●●	●● $\neq$ ✋(5)	6 $\neq$ 5 + 2
3 $=$ ○○○	○ $=$ ✊	9 $\neq$ 3 + 4
1 $\neq$ ●●	●● $\neq$ ✋(4)	7 $=$ 1 + 6
4 $\neq$ ●●●●●	●●●●● $=$ ✋(5)	8 $=$ 4 + 4

Count and write how many. Ring **fewer**.

3	(2)

Write the numbers from 11 through 30.

11									

Tens in Teen Numbers: A Game

10

11

My
Unit 5
Teen Number
Book

By _____

For 10 and 11, draw that many things and circle 10.

12

13

14

15

For 12, 13, 14, and 15, draw that many things and circle 10.

16

17

18

19

For 16, 17, 18, and 19, draw that many things and circle 10.

10 =

Partners of 10: Class Project **239**

10 =

Partners of 10: Class Project

Class Activity

Name _____

9 + 1

8 + 2

7 + 3

6 + 4

5 + 5

4 + 6

3 + 7

2 + 8

1 + 9

© Houghton Mifflin Harcourt Publishing Company

1. Write the 10-partners in order.

2. Write the 10-partners in order.

3. Write the 10-partners in order.

UNIT 5 LESSON 12

Partners of 10: Class Project **241**

Subtract the numbers.

2 − 2 = ☐

3 − 1 = ☐

4 − 1 = ☐

5 − 4 = ☐

5 − 1 = ☐

3 − 2 = ☐

2 − 1 = ☐

3 − 1 = ☐

5 − 3 = ☐

3 − 3 = ☐

5 − 4 = ☐

5 − 2 = ☐

4 − 0 = ☐

2 − 1 = ☐

4 − 2 = ☐

10 − 4 = ☐

10 − 3 = ☐

7 − 4 = ☐

6 − 3 = ☐

9 − 2 = ☐

8 − 4 = ☐

6 − 5 = ☐

6 − 4 = ☐

7 − 2 = ☐

6 − 1 = ☐

10 − 2 = ☐

8 − 2 = ☐

Partners of 10: Class Project

Partners of 7

6 + 1

5 + 2

4 + 3

3 + 4

2 + 5

1 + 6

+

+

+

+

+

+

+

+

+

+

+

+

1. Write the 7-partners in order.

2. Write the 7-partners in order.

3. Write the 7-partners in order.

4. Write the 7-partners in order.

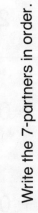

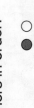

© Houghton Mifflin Harcourt Publishing Company

Name _____

Add the numbers.

$1 + 1 = \boxed{}$ $3 + 3 = \boxed{}$ $8 + 2 = \boxed{}$

$1 + 2 = \boxed{}$ $4 + 4 = \boxed{}$ $7 + 2 = \boxed{}$

$2 + 1 = \boxed{}$ $6 + 3 = \boxed{}$ $6 + 4 = \boxed{}$

$2 + 5 = \boxed{}$ $5 + 2 = \boxed{}$ $5 + 0 = \boxed{}$

$1 + 6 = \boxed{}$ $7 + 1 = \boxed{}$ $6 + 0 = \boxed{}$

$2 + 8 = \boxed{}$ $6 + 1 = \boxed{}$ $2 + 1 = \boxed{}$

$5 + 3 = \boxed{}$ $5 + 2 = \boxed{}$ $4 + 4 = \boxed{}$

$5 + 4 = \boxed{}$ $9 + 0 = \boxed{}$ $4 + 5 = \boxed{}$

$6 + 2 = \boxed{}$ $8 + 0 = \boxed{}$ $7 + 3 = \boxed{}$

Introduction to Counting and Grouping Routines

VOCABULARY
equal

Match. Add shapes to make the two groups **equal**.
Write the number and the partners.

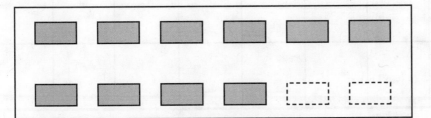

6
_____

4 + 2
_____

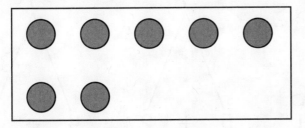

_____

_____

_____

_____

_____

_____

_____

_____

_____

_____

1. Write the numbers 1 through 20.

1									
11									

2. Draw Tiny Tumblers on the Math Mountains. Discuss the way the numbers in the partners change.

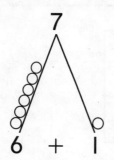   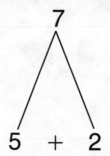   

7   7   7

6 + 1   5 + 2   4 + 3

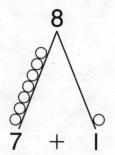   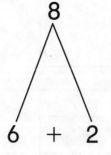      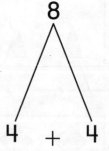

8   8   8   8

7 + 1   6 + 2   5 + 3   4 + 4

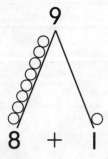   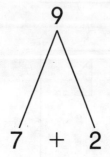   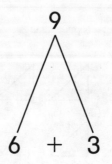   

9   9   9   9

8 + 1   7 + 2   6 + 3   5 + 4

Name _____

Draw Tiny Tumblers. Write how many there are on each Math Mountain.

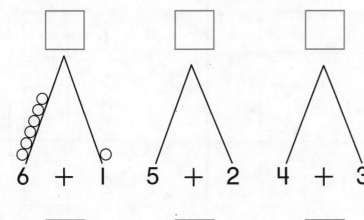

6 + 1   5 + 2   4 + 3

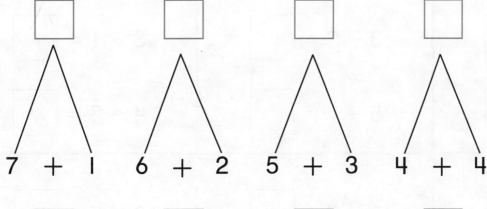

7 + 1   6 + 2   5 + 3   4 + 4

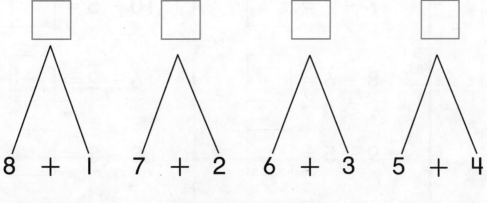

8 + 1   7 + 2   6 + 3   5 + 4

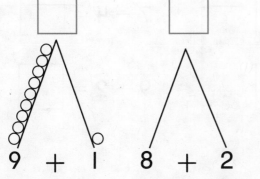 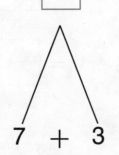 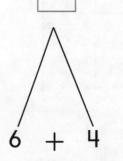 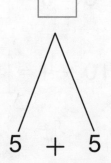

9 + 1   8 + 2   7 + 3   6 + 4   5 + 5

© Houghton Mifflin Harcourt Publishing Company

Subtract the numbers.

$5 - 3 = \boxed{}$ $2 - 0 = \boxed{}$ $4 - 1 = \boxed{}$

$3 - 3 = \boxed{}$ $5 - 4 = \boxed{}$ $1 - 0 = \boxed{}$

$4 - 2 = \boxed{}$ $2 - 1 = \boxed{}$ $5 - 2 = \boxed{}$

$5 - 4 = \boxed{}$ $3 - 2 = \boxed{}$ $3 - 1 = \boxed{}$

$4 - 4 = \boxed{}$ $5 - 1 = \boxed{}$ $4 - 3 = \boxed{}$

$9 - 6 = \boxed{}$ $7 - 2 = \boxed{}$ $10 - 5 = \boxed{}$

$7 - 4 = \boxed{}$ $8 - 6 = \boxed{}$ $6 - 2 = \boxed{}$

$10 - 2 = \boxed{}$ $9 - 5 = \boxed{}$ $8 - 3 = \boxed{}$

$8 - 5 = \boxed{}$ $6 - 3 = \boxed{}$ $7 - 4 = \boxed{}$

$10 - 4 = \boxed{}$ $8 - 4 = \boxed{}$ $9 - 2 = \boxed{}$

Add Partners to Find Totals

Name _____

Write the numbers and compare them.

Write G for **Greater** and L for **Less**.

Cross out from the greater number to make the groups **equal**.

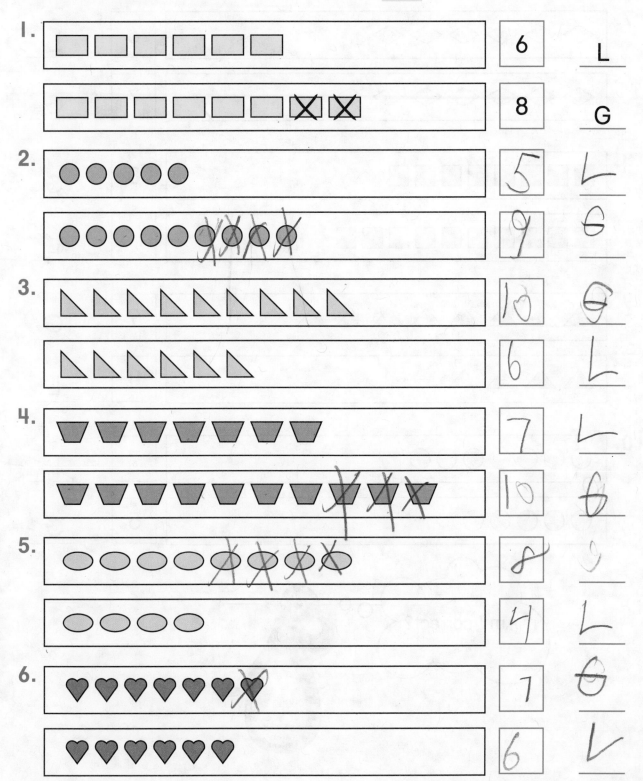

1. 6   L
    8   G

2. 5   L
    9   G

3. 10 G
    6   L

4. 7   L
    10 G

5. 8   G
    4   L

6. 7   G
    6   L

Name _____

Puzzled Penguin compared groups,
 writing G for Greater and L for Less.
Check Puzzled Penguin's answers.

7.  | 6 | L ✓

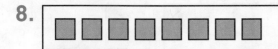 | 7 | G

8.  | 8̶ | G̶ L

 | 10 | L̶ 6

9.  | 9 | G ✓

 | 4 | L

10. 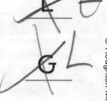 | 7 | L̶ G

 | 5 | G L

Am I correct?

Story Problems and Comparing: Totals Through 10

Write the numbers and compare them. Write G for **Greater** and
L for **Less**. Add (draw more) to make the groups **equal**.

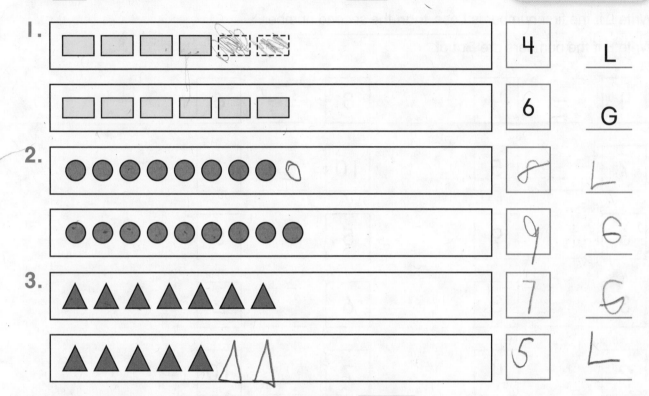

1. 4   L

    6   G

2. 8   L

    9   G

3. 7   G

    5   L

Write the numbers and compare them. Write G for **Greater** and
L for **Less**. Subtract (cross out) to make the groups **equal**.

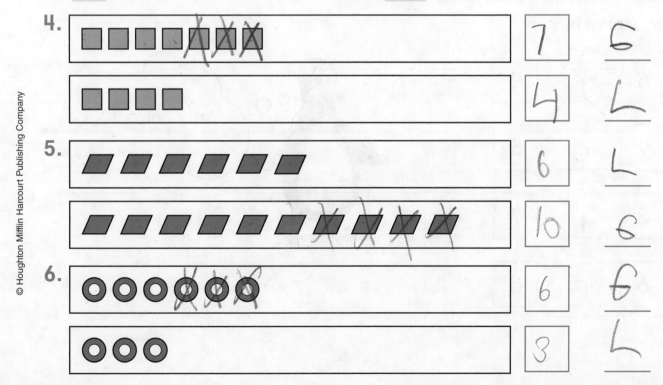

4. 7   G

    4   L

5. 6   L

    10   G

6. 6   G

    3   L

VOCABULARY
greater than
less than
equal

Compare the numbers.

Write G if the first number is **Greater than** the second number.

Write L if the first number is **Less than** the second number.

Write E if the numbers are **Equal**.

4	E	4		8	G	6
7	G	5		10	G	1
6	L	9		5	E	5
3	E	3		6	G	2
2	L	4		7	L	10

Look at Puzzled Penguin's answers.

Help Puzzled Penguin.

6	~~G~~ L	4
9	G	5
3	L	7
6	~~G~~	8

Am I correct?

Subtract to Make Equal Groups

5-18

Class Activity

Name ________________

VOCABULARY
teen number

Write how many more than ten.

Draw circles to show each **teen number**.

11 = 10 + 1

○	○	○	○	○	○	○	○	○	○	○									

12 = 10 + 2

○	○	○	○	○	○	○	○	○	○	○	○								

13 = 10 + 3

○	○	○	○	○	○	○	○	○	○	○	○	○							

14 = 10 + 4

○	○	○	○	○	○	○	○	○	○	○	○	○	○						

15 = 10 + 5

○	○	○	○	○	○	○	○	○	○	○	○	○	○	○					

16 = 10 + 6

○	○	○	○	○	○	○	○	○	○	○	○	○	○	○	○				

17 = 10 + 7

○	○	○	○	○	○	○	○	○	○	○	○	○	○	○	○	○			

18 = 10 + 8

○	○	○	○	○	○	○	○	○	○	○	○	○	○	○	○	○	○		

19 = 10 + 9

○	○	○	○	○	○	○	○	○	○	○	○	○	○	○	○	○	○	○	

10   6

$10 = 9 + 1$ $10 = 1 + 9$ $6 = 5 + 1$

$10 = 8 + 2$ $10 = 2 + 8$ $6 = 1 + 5$

$10 = 7 + 3$ $10 = 3 + 7$ $6 = 4 + 2$

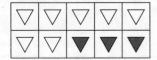

$10 = 6 + 4$ $10 = 4 + 6$ $6 = 2 + 4$

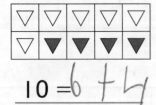   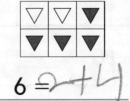

$10 = 5 + 5$ $10 = 5 + 5$ $6 = 3 + 3$

Subtract the numbers.

5 − 3 = ☐	4 − 4 = ☐	4 − 2 = ☐
5 − 4 = ☐	5 − 2 = ☐	5 − 1 = ☐
3 − 1 = ☐	3 − 2 = ☐	4 − 0 = ☐
4 − 3 = ☐	2 − 1 = ☐	5 − 5 = ☐
2 − 2 = ☐	4 − 1 = ☐	2 − 0 = ☐

9 − 1 = ☐	8 − 1 = ☐	9 − 5 = ☐
7 − 2 = ☐	10 − 5 = ☐	6 − 1 = ☐
10 − 1 = ☐	9 − 4 = ☐	10 − 3 = ☐
8 − 4 = ☐	6 − 2 = ☐	9 − 2 = ☐

Name _____

Subtract the numbers.

3 − 2 = ☐   2 − 1 = ☐   2 − 0 = ☐

1 − 1 = ☐   3 − 1 = ☐   4 − 2 = ☐

5 − 4 = ☐   5 − 0 = ☐   5 − 3 = ☐

4 − 1 = ☐   4 − 3 = ☐   4 − 0 = ☐

5 − 2 = ☐   4 − 4 = ☐   5 − 1 = ☐

8 − 5 = ☐   9 − 3 = ☐   6 − 4 = ☐

7 − 4 = ☐   6 − 2 = ☐   10 − 5 = ☐

10 − 2 = ☐   7 − 5 = ☐   9 − 5 = ☐

10 − 3 = ☐   8 − 4 = ☐   9 − 2 = ☐

Tens and Ones

Name _____

© Houghton Mifflin Harcourt Publishing Company

Draw circles to show each number.
Write ten and the extra ones under the circles.
Complete the equations on the bottom.

11	12	13	14	15	16	17	18	19	20
$10+1$	$10+$	$10+$	$+$	$+$	$+$	$+$	$+$	$+$	$+$

$$14 = 10 + \text{\_\_\_}$$
$$15 = 10 + \text{\_\_\_}$$
$$12 = 10 + \text{\_\_\_}$$
$$13 = 10 + \text{\_\_\_}$$
$$17 = 10 + \text{\_\_\_}$$
$$19 = 10 + \text{\_\_\_}$$
$$16 = 10 + \text{\_\_\_}$$
$$18 = 10 + \text{\_\_\_}$$

Subtract the numbers.

$2 - 1 =$ ☐ $5 - 4 =$ ☐ $4 - 2 =$ ☐

$5 - 3 =$ ☐ $4 - 3 =$ ☐ $5 - 1 =$ ☐

$3 - 0 =$ ☐ $3 - 1 =$ ☐ $2 - 2 =$ ☐

$3 - 2 =$ ☐ $5 - 3 =$ ☐ $1 - 0 =$ ☐

$5 - 4 =$ ☐ $3 - 3 =$ ☐ $5 - 2 =$ ☐

$7 - 4 =$ ☐ $9 - 5 =$ ☐ $7 - 1 =$ ☐

$9 - 2 =$ ☐ $10 - 5 =$ ☐ $9 - 3 =$ ☐

$6 - 4 =$ ☐ $8 - 5 =$ ☐ $8 - 3 =$ ☐

$9 - 1 =$ ☐ $8 - 4 =$ ☐ $7 - 5 =$ ☐

Teen Numbers, Partners, and Equations

Dear Family:

In the next two lessons, your child will be learning how to compare several measurable attributes of objects, including length, height, and weight. They will also learn how to compare the capacity of containers.

Your child will use the words *longer* and *shorter* to compare the lengths of two objects and the words *taller* and *shorter* to compare heights. You can help your child by practicing these comparisons at home. For example, while having a meal, you might ask your child which is taller, the table or the chair. If your child is drawing, you can ask him or her to compare the lengths of two different crayons. Young children have better success comparing length when the two objects are aligned, as shown here.

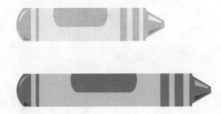

Your child will also be learning to compare weight and capacity. These comparisons may also be practiced at home. You might ask your child to hold a toy in each hand and say which is *heavier* and which is *lighter*. They will be shown that bigger does not always mean heavier. A pillow, for example, may be lighter than a book that is smaller.

Comparisons of capacity can be practiced at mealtime. You might ask your child to say which holds *more* and which holds *less*, the carton of milk or the drinking glass.

Sincerely,
Your child's teacher

COMMON CORE
Unit 5 includes the Common Core Standards for Mathematical Content for Counting and Cardinality K.CC.1, K.CC.2, K.CC.3, K.CC.4, K.CC.4a, K.CC.4b, K.CC.4c, K.CC.5; Operations and Algebraic Thinking K.OA.1, K.OA.2, K.OA.3; Measurement and Data K.MD.1, K.MD.2 and all Mathematical Practices.

Estimada familia:

En las siguientes dos lecciones, su niño aprenderá cómo comparar varios atributos que pueden medirse en los objetos, incluyendo la longitud, la altura y el peso. También aprenderá cómo comparar la capacidad de diferentes recipientes.

Su niño usará los términos *más largo* y *más corto* para comparar la longitud de dos objetos, y los términos *más alto* y *más bajo*, para comparar las alturas. Puede ayudar a su niño practicando estas comparaciones en casa. Por ejemplo, mientras comen, puede preguntarle, cuál es más alta, la mesa o la silla. Si su niño está dibujando, puede pedirle que compare la longitud de dos crayones diferentes. A los niños se les hace más fácil comparar la longitud si los dos objetos que comparan están alineados, como se muestra aquí.

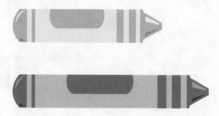

Su niño también aprenderá a comparar peso y capacidad. Estas comparaciones también pueden practicarse en casa. Puede pedirle que sostenga un juguete en cada mano y que diga cuál es *más pesado* y cuál es *más liviano*. Se le enseñará que más grande no siempre quiere decir más pesado. Una almohada, por ejemplo, puede ser más liviana que un libro pequeño.

Las comparaciones de capacidad se pueden practicar a la hora de la comida. Puede pedir a su niño que diga cuál contiene *más* y cuál contiene *menos*, el envase de leche o el vaso.

Atentamente,
El maestro de su niño

COMMON CORE La Unidad 5 incluye los Common Core Standards for Mathematical Content for Counting and Cardinality K.CC.1, K.CC.2, K.CC.3, K.CC.4, K.CC.4a, K.CC.4b, K.CC.4c, K.CC.5; Operations and Algebraic Thinking K.OA.1, K.OA.2, K.OA.3; Measurement and Data K.MD.1, K.MD.2 and all Mathematical Practices.

More Tens in Teen Numbers: A Game

Name _____

VOCABULARY
greater
less
equal

Write the numbers and compare them. Write G for **Greater** and L for **Less**. Add (draw more) to make the groups **equal**.

1. 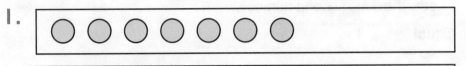 | 7 | G

 | 4 | L

2. 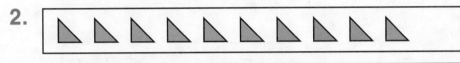 | ☐ | ___

 | ☐ | ___

3.  | ☐ | ___

 | ☐ | ___

Write the numbers and compare them. Write G for **Greater** and L for **Less**. Subtract (cross out) to make the groups **equal**.

4. 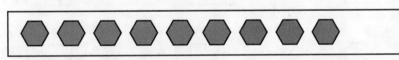 | ☐ | ___

 | ☐ | ___

5. 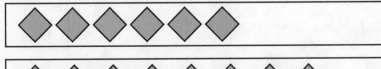 | ☐ | ___

 | ☐ | ___

6. ☐ | ___

☐ | ___

Name _____

Compare the numbers.

Write G if the first number is **Greater than** the second number.

Write L if the first number is **Less than** the second number.

Write E if the numbers are **Equal**.

5	E	5		7	___	6
2	___	7		2	___	2
10	___	4		9	___	4
3	___	4		5	___	8
8	___	8		2	___	3
5	___	9		6	___	10
8	___	6		4	___	4
7	___	1		6	___	2

More Tens in Teen Numbers: A Game

Name _____

VOCABULARY
shorter
taller

Circle the **taller** animal.
Draw a line under the **shorter** animal.

1.

2.

3.

4.

Circle the **longer** fish.
Draw a line under the **shorter** fish.

5.

6.

7.

8.

© Houghton Mifflin Harcourt Publishing Company • Image Credits: (pink Squarespot) ©WaterFrame/Getty Images; (orange Garibaldi) ©Corbis; (yellow fish) ©Dina Ahmed Tarkhan/Flickr/Getty Images; (striped wrasse) ©Gerald Nowak/Westend61/Corbis

Exercise 1. Draw.

Draw a picture to show 10 ones and 4 ones.

Exercises 2–4. Write how many more than ten. Draw circles to show the teen number.

16 = 10 + ____

17 = 10 + ____

18 = 10 + ____

Exercises 5–6. Circle ten. Write ten and the extra ones in each equation.

_____ + _____ = _____   _____ + _____ = _____

Exercises 7–10. Write the partners for 5.

_____ + _____   _____ + _____   _____ + _____   _____ + _____

Exercises 11–15. Write the partners for 10.

_____ + _____   _____ + _____   _____ + _____   _____ + _____   _____ + _____

Exercises 16–18. Add.

$7 + 2 =$ ☐ $4 + 3 =$ ☐ $9 + 1 =$ ☐

Exercises 19–21. Subtract.

$8 - 4 =$ ☐ $10 - 2 =$ ☐ $6 - 3 =$ ☐

Exercise 22. Write the numbers and compare them.
Write **G** for **Greater** and **L** for **Less**.
Cross out to make the groups equal.

 ☐ ___

 ☐ ___

Exercise 23. Circle the longer object.

Exercise 24. Circle the lighter object.

Exercise 25. Extended Response Draw to solve. Then write the equation.

There are 5 horses in the field.

Then 2 more horses come to the field.

How many horses are in the field altogether?

Equation: _____